GEMS

FROM

THE

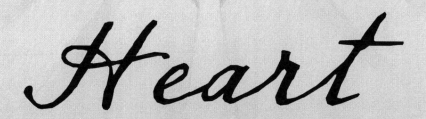

Heart

RUTH R PAYNE

COVER ARTWORK BY AMBER KENNISON

WestBow Press®
A DIVISION OF THOMAS NELSON
& ZONDERVAN

Copyright © 2023 Ruth R Payne.

All rights reserved. No part of this book may be used or reproduced by any means, graphic, electronic, or mechanical, including photocopying, recording, taping or by any information storage retrieval system without the written permission of the author except in the case of brief quotations embodied in critical articles and reviews.

This book is a work of non-fiction. Unless otherwise noted, the author and the publisher make no explicit guarantees as to the accuracy of the information contained in this book and in some cases, names of people and places have been altered to protect their privacy.

WestBow Press books may be ordered through booksellers or by contacting:

WestBow Press
A Division of Thomas Nelson & Zondervan
1663 Liberty Drive
Bloomington, IN 47403
www.westbowpress.com
844-714-3454

Because of the dynamic nature of the Internet, any web addresses or links contained in this book may have changed since publication and may no longer be valid. The views expressed in this work are solely those of the author and do not necessarily reflect the views of the publisher, and the publisher hereby disclaims any responsibility for them.

Any people depicted in stock imagery provided by Getty Images are models, and such images are being used for illustrative purposes only.
Certain stock imagery © Getty Images.

Cover artwork by Amber Kennison
Interior Image Credit: Ruth Payne; Anna Payne; Esther Milner

ISBN: 978-1-6642-9880-4 (sc)
ISBN: 978-1-6642-9881-1 (e)

Library of Congress Control Number: 2023907957

Print information available on the last page.

WestBow Press rev. date: 05/01/2023

CONTENTS

Dedication vii

Bleeding Hearts 1
Precious Jewels 2
The Road 3
God's Light 4
Even Teddy Bears Sleep 5
Fear or Trust 6
God Cares 7
Be Still 8
Perfect Peace 9
God's Love 10
Nothing can Separate 11
Hope Thou in the Lord 12
Liberia 13
Lead Me to the Rock 14
I Am Weary 15
I Thank the Lord 16
My Times are in Thy Hands 17
Rain 18
Send Me 19
The Goodness of God 20
Wings Like a Dove 21
You are Protected 22
Beyond the Storm 23
I Cannot See 24
My God is in Control 25
Sisters Forever 26
Thou God Seest Me 27
Thy Word Shall Lead Me 28
My Prayer 29
God Made Mothers 30
The Perfect Gift 31
Friends 32
Tiny Things 33
I will Praise Him Anyway 34
Life's Road 35
My Guide 36

Mikayla	37
God has a Plan	38
Guard Your Heart	39
Through the Eyes of a Child	40
Speak with Love	41
Morning	42
The Door of Heaven	43
Chaos vs. Calmness	44
New Beginnings	45
Have a Safe Christmas	46
About the Author	47

DEDICATION

To my parents, Verle and Anna Payne, for their love and encouragement, for bringing me up with the truth of God's Word, and for teaching me to give my heart, soul, and mind to the work of Christ.

To my best friend, Amber Kennison, for all her support and for the lovely artwork on the front cover.

Bleeding Hearts

Bleeding hearts are a forest flower
That I found while walking through a sunny bower.
Their cheerful colors, all pink and red,
Were opposite their name so full of dread.

And though some grow in a well-known place;
Others are very hard to trace.
They made me think of our land so sweet;
That's also filled with sorrow and deceit.

The bleeding hearts in the life of man
Are filled with sadness and grief and can
Lead to bitterness and rejecting the Lord,
When not everything on His alter is poured.

And sometimes in our own great woe,
We fail to see or even to know
That there are others suffering grief
And waiting for some kind, helpful relief.

Their husband has left them; Their child has died.
Their son is in prison, by jury been tried.
Their mother has cancer and not long to live.
They lost their job; the world has nothing to give.

There is absolutely no hope they think,
And they in grief and despair do sink.
They're waiting for someone to see and to hear
Their silent appeal, their grief and tear.

So those of us who have suffered loss,
Should take all our grievances to the cross,
And there we should leave them with Jesus the Son,
Who has made atonement for everyone.

Then go where we're needed most.
Whether here or on some far coast.
Lend a caring hand to a bleeding heart;
Show them God's path: this is our part.

Help those grieving ones find joy in the Lord.
Help those bleeding hearts all over the world
Find the peace and joy we've discovered
And the wonderful treasure we've uncovered.

When at the cross, we our grief laid
To come to someone else's aid,
So, they too may find at the Savior's feet
New life and joy and peace so sweet.

Ruth Payne

Precious Jewels

I hold in my hand a precious jewel,
An emerald, so green.
A gorgeous ruby, sparkling red,
More beautiful I haven't seen.

I hold in my hand a precious jewel,
An amethyst of lovely hue.
A dazzling sapphire, such deep blue,
That it shines though old or new.

I hold in my arms a precious jewel,
A child, to God so dear.
Somebodies precious bundle of joy,
Whose laugh and cry they always hear.

I hold in my hands a precious jewel,
Just a Book, a wonderful Book.
God's word to tell me how to live
And how the Savior my sin took.

God holds in His hands a precious jewel,
A pearl of great price.
And that is me because I am
A beautiful child of Christ.

Ruth Payne

The Road

Twisty, turvy
Oh, so curvy
Was the road I traveled on.

Bending, binding
Ever winding
'Round the hills of sin and woe.

Grasping, strangling
So, entangling
That my feet knew not the way.

Darkness, fear
So bold and drear
That my heart cried out for light.

Broken, shattered,
Ruined, and scattered
This was all I had to offer.

Loving, dying
Not denying
Jesus Christ the sacrifice.

Kindness, grace
Gentle of face
This was He who took my hand.

Trails increase
Contentment, peace
This my Savior did impart.

Straight, non-altering
Occasionally faltering
Is the road I walk with God.

Bringing, showing
God's love bestowing
As I help my fellowman.

Telling, giving
God's Word living
So they may walk along with me.

Ruth Payne

God's Light

I'm in a world that's black as night,
Where all its people cry for light.
To them there is no hope at all,
And so, they vainly fret and call

But as for me, I have the light
That glows around me in that night.
For it was at the cross I found
God's pardoning love to all around.

This is the hope I want to share
To dying people everywhere.
Oh sinner, won't you see and hear
God's call to you so loud and clear.

Ruth Payne

John 3:16

Even Teddy Bears Sleep

At night I lay down in my bed
My Teddy at my side,
And we close our eyes real tight,
'Till morning to abide.

But our Father up in Heaven,
He never goes to sleep.
He's always watching over us,
From harm and fear to keep.

Thus, our Father we should trust
And not the Teddy Bear.
Because He loves us oh so much
And wants our dreams to share.

Ruth Payne

Proverbs 3:5-6

Fear or Trust

How nice t'would be
To have no fear
To feel no trouble
Drawing near.

But peaceful lives
Without much fuss
Is not what Jesus
Promised us.

He only gives
The needed grace
The challenges each
Day to face.

Lord, help me trust
And have no fear
But lean on You who
Draws me near.

Ruth Payne

God Cares

In this world there are cares,
Grief and sorrow abound.
The evil grows stronger,
And encircles us 'round.

But the Bible it says,
Cast your cares on the Lord.
For His love and His care,
Has for you been outpoured.

Lord, help me to trust You,
Despite all this sadness,
And continue to serve You,
With joy and with gladness.

Ruth Payne

1 Peter 5:7

Be Still

A storm around me rages;
I'm encompassed by a hoard,
But a voice within me whispers
"Be still, I am the Lord".

My soul can find no rest;
Grief wraps 'round me like a cord,
But a voice within me whispers,
"Be still, I am the Lord".

I told the Lord my sorrows,
And my heart to Him I poured,
And a voice within me whispered,
"Be still, I am the Lord".

Now my soul is lifted up;
Like an eagle I have soared,
For a voice within me whispers,
"Be still, I am the Lord.

Ruth Payne

Psalm 46:10a

Perfect Peace

Two beings within me
Are constantly warring.
One pulls me down,
And one sends me soaring.

As long as they're fighting
They give me no peace,
No time to rest,
Or for the storm to cease.

Why do I let these two
Beings destroy me?
My God grants peace;
Trusting Him is the key.

So, one thing I have learned;
Keep your mind on the Lord.
This He has promised;
Perfect Peace for discord.

Ruth Payne

Isaiah 26:3

God's Love

God's love is like an ocean,
Stretching far as I can see.
His love, like ocean waves,
Washes debris away from me.

God's love is like the wind,
Coming to me from on high.
His love, like a soft breeze,
Brings peace to where I lie.

God's love is like the trees,
Sheltering me from Satan's dart.
His love, like the tree's roots,
Reaches deep inside my heart.

God's love abides forever
I will never have to fear.
For He will love me always
And keep and hold me dear.

Ruth Payne

Nothing can Separate

God holds my hand;
I cannot fall.
I'm in His grip;
I've heard His call.

Nothing can loose
The grip He has:
Not things to come
Nor things that pass.

God's love is strong:
His hold stays tight.
He guides me through
The darkening night.

I'll trust His grip
Through stormy vails,
Because I know
God never fails.

Ruth Payne

Hope Thou in the Lord

My soul is cast down
And my spirit's depressed.
My heart cries for peace,
My whole being for rest.

Have I been forgotten
And remembered no more?
I must discover
The peace my soul longs for.

Hope thou in the Lord,
A voice whispers to me,
And be not cast down,
For the light you will see.

So, my tears are gone
And my heart has found peace.
For the Lord heard my cry
And made my sorrows to cease.

Ruth Payne

Psalm 42:11

Liberia

The countryside is so green and lush
With a beautiful blue sky above.
The sun shines with great warmth and brilliance
Filling my heart with God's peace and love.

But beyond all this beauty and light,
I see people who live with great fear
Far away from God's peace and God's love,
With no one to see their grief and tear.

May they see that God really loves them
By the beauty He's placed all around,
And may they give their lives to the Lord
So that light in their hearts may be found.

Ruth Payne

Lead Me to the Rock

Hear my cry, oh Lord,
My heart is broken;
Attend to my prayer,
Which I have spoken.

My most special friend
Has deeply hurt me;
I cannot revive,
Grief's all I can see.

Lead me to the rock
That's higher than I;
Be Thou my shelter
Let sorrow pass by.

So will I sing praise
To You forever,
And trust in Your love
Which does not waver.

Ruth Payne

Psalm 61:2

I Am Weary

Dear Lord, I am weary
And unable to stand.
Discouragement and care
Wrap 'round me like a band.

I feel myself sinking
Beneath a heavy load.
I cannot continue
To walk down this hard road.

I need strength from somewhere
And encouragement, too,
That will help me keep on
Serving others and You.

Your Word clearly tells us
To not become weary,
For in the due season
Reaping will be ready.

Lord, I pray for the strength
To keep marching forward
And also, for courage
To have faith in Your Word.

Ruth Payne

Galations 6:9

I Thank the Lord

I thank the Lord
For all He's made,
And how the earth
He has arrayed.

With butterflies
And birds and trees,
With air and sky
And clouds and bees.

With little goats
Who romp and play,
And little lambs
Who go astray.

With tall mountains
And deep valleys,
With hot deserts
And vast prairies.

With lakes and streams
Sparkling and clear,
Seas and rivers
Both far and near.

With sun and moon
And stars so bright,
With planets, too,
Oh, what a sight.

The human race:
Man, woman, child,
In God's image
We were styled.

All this beauty
Dwells around us,
Yet still evil
Lurks with malice.

Folks are dying
Without the Lord;
Their souls are lost
To hell's discord.

Lord, help me see
Their serious need
Show them God's love
In word and deed.

And through the things
That You have made
Guide them to You
As You have bade.

Ruth Payne

My Times are in Thy Hands

Oh Lord, I know my days are few
My times are in Thy hands.
Help me to use each blessed hour
Thy grace to understand.

And help me, Lord, to show the world
Thy majesty divine
And point them to the only One
Who gives them life sublime.

Ruth Payne

Rain

Today the sky
Is cloudy and gray;
The rain pours down
Obscuring the day.

Tears fill my eyes
As darkness creeps in;
My joy is gone
As though ne'er has been.

I know that rain
In each life must fall
To help us hear
And answer God's call.

Lord, help me see
The brightness each day
Despite the rain
You have sent my way.

And give me strength
To keep praising You,
Thus turning rain
Into sunshine, too.

Ruth Payne

"Into each life some rain must fall".
Henry Wadsworth Longfellow

Send Me

The Lord said, "Go!"
"But Father why?
I like my life."
This was my cry.

"'Cause I need you
To help save souls,
Whose hearts are dark
And black as coals."

"I'd rather not
Go somewhere far.
I love my friends,
And like my car."

My Father said,
"All right, that's fine,
But I will give
To you a sign."

"You say you love
Your fancy car,
Then it I shall
Mess up and mar."

"Then you will know
That life is short,
Material wealth
Of no report."

"And willingly
You'll go for Me,
And where you are
There I will be."

My Father did
Just as He said,
And down His path
My feet He led.

So I did yield
My heart to Him,
My very soul
And life and limb.

"Whom shall I send?"
My Lord did plead.
"Lord, here am I
Send me indeed."

Ruth Payne

Isaiah 6:8

The Goodness of God

Dear God, my heart is full;
Your goodness never fails!
Your mercy reaches far
Calming our stormy gales.

When we learn to trust You
And lay our burdens down,
You, with loving-kindness,
Will trade them for a crown.

I will praise You, oh God,
For Your marvelous ways
And keep on serving You
To the end of my days!

Ruth Payne

Wings Like a Dove

Oh, that I had wings like a dove,
For I would fly away and rest!
I would soar above the heavens
And then return safe to my nest.

Oh, that I had feet like a deer
For I would dash through field and vale!
I would graze by the still waters
And tread on a peaceful trail.

Oh, that I had fins like a fish,
For I would swim through the blue waves!
I would explore the ocean depths
And dwell in dark, seaweed lined caves.

Whatever I may be or do,
The Lord is with me forever
And He will guide all my footsteps;
His great love will leave me never.

Ruth Payne

Psalm 55:6

You are Protected

"You are protected
And quite safe don't you see?"
Was the clear, bold statement
My computer sent me.

But am I as safe
As it has asserted,
Or have I opened files
That have been perverted?

This brings to my mind
Another protection,
Stronger than all others
With safety quite certain.

"You are protected,"
My Lord whispered to me.
"And in My loving hand
Always safe you will be."

Ruth Payne

Beyond the Storm

All around the storm clouds billow,
And yet ahead I see
A sweet haven bright and sunny,
Waiting there for me.

So, I'll ignore the storm around
And look instead to Thee,
My gracious Savior and my Lord,
Standing there for me.

Ruth Payne

I Cannot See

I cannot see the wind
Roaring through the skies,
And yet I know it's there
'Cause through the trees it sighs.

I cannot see the heat
Coming from the sun,
And yet I know it's there
With warmth that equals none.

I cannot see the air
Flowing 'round the world,
And yet I know it's there
With every breath unfurled.

I cannot see ahead;
My future is unclear,
And yet I know God's there
Waiting to draw me near.

I cannot see my Lord,
My Savior and my King,
And yet I know He's there
Controlling everything.

Ruth Payne

My God is in Control

My God is in control;
I will not be forsaken!
He guides my every step
And knows the paths I've taken.

He holds me in His hands
And will never let me go!
God's word I fully trust
His will for me to show.

My God is in control;
I will rest in this His Word!
And trust that He knows best
To guide my life hence forward.

Ruth Payne

Sisters Forever

Sisters are a gift from God.
No price enough, here or abroad,
Could buy the love and loyalty
Sisters bring to a family.

My sister is my best friend,
Whom I would never give or lend.
If you don't have one that's too bad,
'Cause sisters make one very glad.

My dear sister, I love you,
And will always to you be true.
My loyalty will never bend
And my support will never end.

Though the miles between us grow,
It makes no difference here below,
Because we shall forever be
Sisters throughout eternity.

Ruth Payne

Thou God Seest Me

Thou God seest me
Though I am very small,
And everything around me
Seems so very tall.

Thou God seest me
When I have disobeyed,
And done something to grieve You
With mistakes I've made.

Thou God seest me
When I have lost my way,
And when night has drifted in
Blotting out the day.

Thou God seest me
No matter where I go,
And in Your hands You'll hold me
Your love to fully show.

Ruth Payne

Genesis 16:13a

Thy Word Shall Lead Me

Thy light shall surely guide my way;
Thy lamp my steps shall show.
Thy Word shall lead me in the path
Where Thou wouldst have me go.

Thy loving hand shall hold me tight;
Thy grip shall never fail.
I'll trust Thy Word through peaceful times
And through the stormy vale.

Ruth Payne

Psalm 119:105

My Prayer

Oh God, I lift Your name on high
And praise You as the days go by.
I know Your kingdom soon shall come
And that there's room for everyone.

Thank You today for daily bread
And for supplies in days ahead.
Forgive us now the wrongs we've made
As we forgive as You have bade.

And in temptation lead us not
But let all evil be forgot.
Thine is the kingdom here we know
Power and glory is Yours below.

Ruth Payne

Paraphrase of the Lord's Prayer
Matthew 6:9-13

God Made Mothers

God made mothers
To patch up our knees
And comfort our woes
Of various degrees.

God made mothers
To teach us the right
And how to behave
When out of her sight.

God made mothers,
I know this is true,
And I'm glad He made
A mother like you.

Ruth Payne

Proverbs 31:10, 28a

The Perfect Gift

Some folks have everything
This life is sure to need.
To find the perfect gift,
My thoughts I must now heed.

The flower will not last;
It will soon fade away.
The candle shrinks in size;
It also will not stay.

The playful puppy dog,
Not everyone will like.
The noisy cockatoo
May make them take a hike.

The gift that's sure to last
Is just a simple phrase:
"I love you, Mother dear,"
Will last for all her days.

Ruth Payne

Can substitute Father and his for Mother and hers in last stanza.

Friends

A friend is someone near,
So very close and dear.
A shoulder to cry on;
There when the day is done.

A friend will listen well
And never tales tell.
In secrets of your heart
They love to be a part.

Friends are a gift from God,
Near home or far abroad.
The Lord I thank hereto
For such a friend like you.

Ruth Payne

Tiny Things

A tiny drop of water
Is all a plant may need,
To grow a mighty root
From such a tiny seed.

A tiny grain of sand
An oyster now may hold,
To form a mighty pearl
More valuable than gold.

A tiny bit of faith
Is all that God requires,
To move a mighty mountain
And set it where one desires.

Ruth Payne

I will Praise Him Anyway

Today I really wondered
If the sky is always gray,
Then in my heart I said
I will praise God anyway.

Oft it seems the sun won't shine
And thick fog is here to stay,
But like the birds above
I will praise God anyway.

No matter how dark it seems
I will always joyful stay;
Try to bring the sunshine in
And praise God anyway.

Ruth Payne

Life's Road

Life's road is often hard
The path not always smooth,
The problems of each day
Make hurts so hard to soothe.

When those around us mock
And treat us so unfair,
It makes the life we lead
So very hard to bear.

It takes away our joy
And causes so much pain;
We long for better days
And life with much less strain.

When times become like this
Our eyes to God must turn;
Our cares we must lay down
His joy and peace to learn.

Ruth Payne
Romans 8:28

My Guide

The Lord's my guide
I will not fear,
For He shall always
Draw me near.

He leads me by
The pastures green,
Where peaceful waters
Flow serene.

My soul the Lord
Daily restores,
In paths of right my
Steps He lures.

When I pass through
Valleys drear,
No evil need I
Now to fear.

His rod and staff,
They comfort me.
For He is near,
Always shall be.

A table God
Has now prepared,
That my enemies
Have not shared.

Over my head
He oil pours;
My cup runs o'er and
My heart soars.

So shall goodness
And mercy true,
Follow me through
All my days new.

And in God's house
Will I now dwell;
Forevermore His
Love to tell.

Ruth Payne

Psalm 23

Mikayla

(Gift from God)

A tiny gift from God,
From open arms now torn.
The Father took you home
Before ere you were born.

Now as we try to think
And know the reason why,
May Jesus hold us close
And listen to our cry.

And help us understand
This gift was far too dear
So Jesus took her home;
In heaven holds her near.

Ruth Payne

Written in Memory of my niece, Mikayla Rose Milner, 9/6/2011.

God has a Plan

God has a plan
For life's dim trail,
And every strong
And stormy gale.

It is not ours
To ask Him why,
Nor fear the darkness
Drawing nigh.

He only asks
For simple trust,
Our cares to leave
With Him a must.

Our hand in His,
No more to fear
For He will guide
Our footsteps here.

Ruth Payne

Guard Your Heart

Abiding in this world
Yet being not a part
Of all the evil things
Dear to Satan's heart.

Observing how my tongue
Might spread a hurtful word,
And how the way I act
May grieve my precious Lord.

Discerning how my eyes
May see a harmful sight,
And always, ever look
Toward things within God's light.

Deciding that my feet
Shall only good paths tread,
And know in conscious thought
No consequence I dread.

Keeping my heart from sin
Since here my Lord doth dwell,
And in this quiet way
My love for Christ will tell.

These things I must control,
The Holy Spirit heed,
To show the world around
The life God's child leads.

Ruth Payne

Proverbs 4:23

Through the Eyes of a Child

I want to view life
Through the eyes of a child.
Find something brand new,
Fresh and undefiled.

Trust God without fail,
Taking all to His Throne,
And without a doubt
Trust His will, not my own.

Give love with no thought
Of any return,
Making blessing my life
Not my own concern.

Lord, give me the grace
To leave all at Thy feet,
And like a small child,
By Your side take a seat.

Ruth Payne

Speak with Love

Speak with love,
And not with hate,
For soon your words
May be too late.

Speak with love;
'Tis better far
Then using words
That hurt and mar.

Speak with love,
This is the way
To turn one's heart
Toward God today.

Speak with love;
'Tis God's command
The world to show
His love firsthand.

Ruth Payne

Morning

The birds are singing cheerfully
At the dawning day.
The skies are slowly turning
To various shades of gray.

And now the sun is peeping
Above the misty hill;
The clouds are gleaming colors
And seemingly so still.

The sun it rises higher;
Mankind begins to wake,
And in the brand-new morning
Their various paths to take.

I thank the Lord for morning,
A precious gift He gave,
Another chance to praise Him
His love to ever crave.

Ruth Payne

The Door of Heaven

Today as I went walking
I had sorrow in my heart.
For my close, loving family
Had just been torn apart.

The Lord today had chosen
To take home an Uncle dear,
Through the Door of Heaven
And we so miss him here.

As along my path I went,
My eyes turned towards the sky
And my gaze was quickly drawn
To the heaven's up so high.

The clouds above had parted,
The sun was shining through
As though the Door of Heaven
Had opened for me too.

My heart then had some comfort
From the beauty of that sight
In knowing that my Uncle
Was safe beyond that light.

And when the Door of Heaven
Will open wide for me
I know that as I enter
My Uncle I will see.

Ruth Payne

Chaos vs. Calmness

The world is full of panic,
Everything is shutting down.
People are becoming ill,
There's chaos all around.

During this tribulation
Please remember this:
The birds, they still are singing;
The sun, we'll never miss.

The mountains, they are calling;
The rivers, still they flow;
The plants, they still are growing;
The ground, still firm below.

Your family, still around you;
God, still in control.
We need to cease the panic
And have calmness be our goal.

Ruth Payne

New Beginnings

The morning comes,
The day grows bright;
A new day dawns
Out of the night.

The rain pours down
The seeds they grow;
A new plant springs
From down below.

Inside the womb
A child's designed;
A new life starts,
Part of mankind.

December comes,
All season's past;
A new year starts,
Time moves so fast.

I thank the Lord
For all His ways;
He makes brand new
All of my days.

Ruth Payne

II Cor. 5:17

Have a Safe Christmas

'Twas the night before Christmas
And on the highways
Folks were all rushing
To their in-laws to stay.

The traffic was bad,
The snow was so deep,
When all of a sudden
Horns started to beep.

Folks slammed on their brakes
But to no avail.
The cars kept on sliding
Into the guard rail.

The State Patrol came,
And the ambulance too.
The fire truck also
With all of its crew.

Folks went to the hospital;
Some were hurt bad.
A few might not make it;
It all seemed so sad.

And so, on this holiday,
Remember this;
Slow down and drive safe
For a Christmas of bliss.

Ruth Payne

ABOUT THE AUTHOR

Ruth Payne was born and raised in Washington State and spent most of her childhood years living on a ranch in rural Eastern Washington. She currently works as an Advanced EMT for an EMS agency in the mountains of North Central Washington. She enjoys spending time doing outside activities which include hiking, biking, and skiing.